THE LAST STAND OF CHUCK NORRIS

ALSO BY IAN SPECTOR

The Truth About Chuck Norris

Chuck Norris vs. Mr. T

Chuck Norris Cannot Be Stopped

400 ALL-NEW FACTS ABOUT THE MOST TERRIFYING MAN IN THE UNIVERSE

by IAN SPECTOR

GOTHAM
BOOKS

THE LAST STAND OF CHUCK NORRIS

GOTHAM BOOKS
Published by Penguin Group (USA) Inc.
375 Hudson Street, New York, New York 10014, U.S.A.
Penguin Group (Canada), 90 Eglinton Avenue East, Suite 700, Toronto, Ontario M4P 2Y3, Canada (a division of Pearson Penguin Canada Inc.); Penguin Books Ltd, 80 Strand, London WC2R 0RL, England; Penguin Ireland, 25 St Stephen's Green, Dublin 2, Ireland (a division of Penguin Books Ltd); Penguin Group (Australia), 250 Camberwell Road, Camberwell, Victoria 3124, Australia (a division of Pearson Australia Group Pty Ltd); Penguin Books India Pvt Ltd, 11 Community Centre, Panchsheel Park, New Delhi–110 017, India; Penguin Group (NZ), 67 Apollo Drive, Rosedale, Auckland 0632, New Zealand (a division of Pearson New Zealand Ltd); Penguin Books (South Africa) (Pty) Ltd, 24 Sturdee Avenue, Rosebank, Johannesburg 2196, South Africa

Penguin Books Ltd, Registered Offices: 80 Strand, London WC2R 0RL, England

Published by Gotham Books, a member of Penguin Group (USA) Inc.

First printing, May 2011
10 9 8 7 6 5 4 3 2 1

LIBRARY OF CONGRESS CATALOGING-IN-PUBLICATION DATA
The last stand of Chuck Norris : 400 all-new facts about the most terrifying man in the universe / Ian Spector.
p. cm
ISBN 978-1-592-40645-6 (pbk.)
1. American wit and humor. 2. Norris, Chuck, 1940—Humor. I. Title.
PN6165.S6783 2011
796.8092—dc22

2011004325

Printed in the United States of America
Set in Caxton Book, Clarendon, and Impact • Designed by Sabrina Bowers

FOR YOU, THE READER:

Present this book for 10% off your next meal at participating IHOP restaurants.*

*Neither my publisher nor I are affiliated with IHOP and their mission to serve delicious breakfast foods at reasonable prices. In fact, most likely, you will not be able to receive a discount at any retail establishment for simply showing up with this book. Regardless, to show my appreciation for your continued patronage, I figured it couldn't hurt to try to improve your day.

THE LAST STAND OF CHUCK NORRIS

Chuck Norris pronounces "ballet" like "ballot," "Arkansas" like "are-Kansas" and "Barack Obama" like "Kenyan socialist."

Toward the end of Super Bowl XLIV, Chuck Norris placed a friendly $1 bet on the New Orleans Saints. Coincidentally, Peyton Manning threw a game-ending interception seconds later.

Chuck Norris once chopped down a cherry tree with his dick. When George Washington's father asked him who chopped down the cherry tree, Chuck Norris responded by banging George Washington's mom. It is for this reason that Chuck Norris is known as "the Grandfather of Our Country."

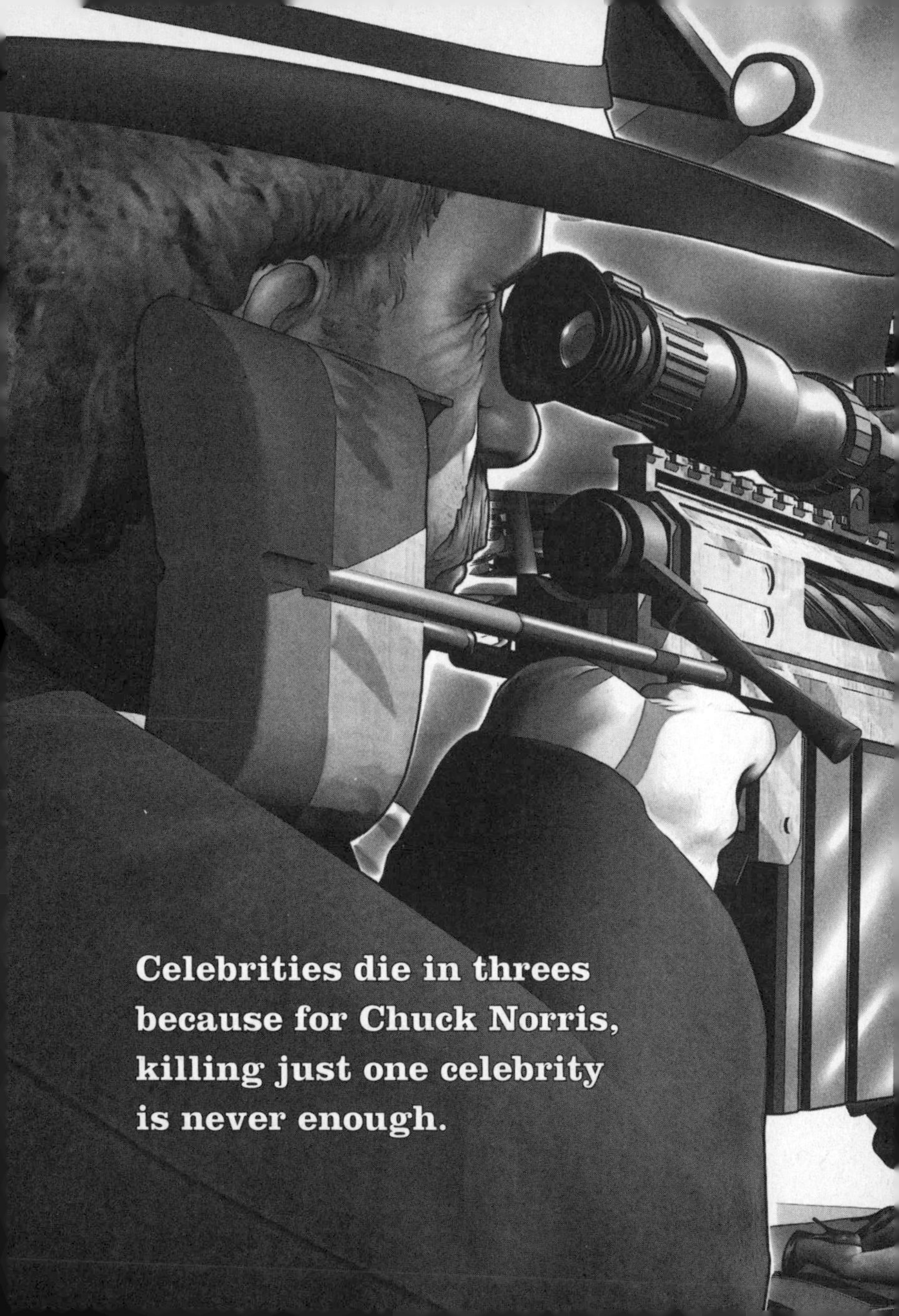

Celebrities die in threes because for Chuck Norris, killing just one celebrity is never enough.

THE 16th ANNUAL
RICH SNOBBY
WHORE
AWARDS
THE 16th ANNUAL
RICH SNOBBY
WHORE
AWARDS
THE 16th ANNUAL
RICH SNOBBY
WHORE
THE 16th ANNUAL
RICH SNOBBY
WHORE
AWARDS

If looks could kill, Chuck Norris would have gouged out one of his eyes years ago just to make it challenging.

The only thing able to cut Chuck Norris's beard is his razor-sharp reflexes.

Chuck Norris's favorite hot dog topping is mustard distilled from the tears of the children of his victims. Chuck Norris eats a lot of hot dogs.

A single hair from Chuck Norris's beard is soft enough to be woven into the softest bedsheets you will ever sleep on, yet strong enough to suspend Wilford Brimley in gale-force winds.

The Total Gym can also grill cheeseburgers, press your pants, and file your taxes, and Chuck Norris can teach you how on twelve incredible DVDs for just seven easy payments of $39.95.

When Chuck Norris plays basketball, his dick gets its own jersey and usually plays for the opposing team.

For an extra kick, Chuck Norris spikes his aftershave with just a splash of battery acid.

Chuck Norris is actually an extremely talented harpsichordist who has brought audiences to tears with his rendition of "Thong Song."

During the Great Rocky Mountain Blackout of 2004, the city of Las Vegas was powered for two days entirely by friction generated on Chuck Norris's beard.

Chuck Norris once broke into a sealed, six-inch-thick lead vault using nothing but a paper clip, a wad of chewing gum, MacGyver's rib cage, and the combination.

When Chuck Norris played for the Dodgers, he wore number 42 and nobody said a word.

Chuck Norris's favorite boot has been up so many asses, it received a lifetime achievement award from the American Society of Proctologists.

Before a dodo shit on Chuck Norris's pickup truck, the dodo was the most common species of bird in the world.

Chuck Norris stuffs his Thanksgiving turkey with a forty-eight-ounce porterhouse steak stuffed inside a Vietnamese prison guard.

The Obama administration originally wanted to send Chuck Norris to clean up the BP oil spill, but they axed the idea after hearing a rumor that crude oil only makes Chuck Norris stronger.

Chuck Norris's nipples can be milked for the smoothest forty-year-aged Texas whiskey you will ever taste.

Chuck Norris's roundhouse kicks have broken over one million bones, but his smile has broken ten times as many hearts.

The sixth leading cause of global warming is the steam wafting off Chuck Norris's urine.

The only reason Chuck Norris has never been elected to any government office is because Chuck Norris *never* runs.

On a road trip when Chuck Norris was eight years old, his father yelled at him, "Don't make me turn this car around!" In response, Chuck punched the backseat so hard, it caused the car to spin a full 180 degrees. He then smirked and said, "Your move, Dad." His father never yelled at him again.

The last time Chuck Norris went to a karaoke bar, he sang Lee Greenwood's "God Bless the USA" and the next day was awarded the Congressional Medal of Honor.

Chuck Norris invented the big bang theory after fucking Albert Einstein's wife.

The only way to tickle Chuck Norris is to douse him in kerosene and light him on fire with a welding torch.

Chuck Norris's toenail clippings are harvested monthly and are the primary ingredient in asphalt.

Chuck Norris's erection is visible from space.

The devil once secretly replaced Chuck Norris's immortal soul with Folgers crystals. Chuck Norris couldn't tell the difference.

Chuck Norris's orgasm has been known to trigger avalanches throughout Europe, volcanic eruptions around the Pacific Rim, and violent political unrest across Tatooine.

In his recent biography, President George W. Bush admits that he never invaded Iran because Chuck Norris told him, "Leave that one for me."

Chuck Norris snores in iambic pentameter.

The only mercy Chuck Norris knows is Mercy Johnson of Topeka, Kansas, because he took her virginity seven times.

The MLB team is called the Texas Rangers only because calling themselves the Texas Walkers seemed like bad mojo for the pitchers.

Chuck Norris retired from competitive tap-dancing after being mistaken by authorities as the epicenter of the 1989 Loma Prieta earthquake.

The Rocky Mountains were created when Chuck Norris pushed California closer to Texas so his flights from Los Angeles to Dallas would take less time.

The original concept for the film *American Beauty* was a shirtless Chuck Norris saluting the flag for two hours.

Chuck Norris is why Pat Sajak's talk show failed.

Chuck Norris's beard is pure matter, and his chest hair is pure antimatter. **IF THE TWO EVER MEET, THE UNIVERSE WILL EXPLODE.**

When Chuck Norris was on Noah's ark, the dragons scuffed his snakeskin boots. That was all it took.

Like many celebrities, Chuck Norris adopts African babies. Except he does it as part of his side project, the World's Biggest Ball of African Babies.

On Ash Wednesday, Chuck Norris's priest says, "Remember, Chuck Norris, that you are awesome."

Chuck Norris's first uncredited role in a movie was as the rabbit in *Monty Python and the Holy Grail*.

Chuck Norris has denim genes.

Chuck Norris's entry in *The Hitchhiker's Guide to the Galaxy* reads simply, "Panic."

Chuck Norris's week is only six days long because he refuses to recognize Tuesday.

On a good day, there is another side of Chuck Norris, a gentler, more feminine side. Chuck Norris hasn't had any good days yet.

Chuck Norris tattooed his name on his fist so it would be the last thing his victims saw.

Before Chuck Norris came to Middle-earth, Hobbits were twelve feet tall.

Chuck Norris once put a thousand monkeys at a thousand typewriters for a thousand years to see if they would, in fact, turn out the complete works of Shakespeare. Unfortunately, they were only able to compose the screenplay for *Delta Force 2: The Colombian Connection.*

In 2008, Chuck Norris won the FINA Water Polo World League Tournament entirely on horseback.

Chuck Norris's semen cures AIDS but causes Alzheimer's disease. HIV-positive women he bangs live for a long time, but they don't remember why.

Chuck Norris knows we put a man on the moon because Chuck Norris was the one who threw him there.

2 12
BELIEVE

The Good, The Bad, and The Ugly are Chuck Norris's nicknames for his testicles.

Chuck Norris was inducted into the Baseball Hall of Fame for ordering a Denny's Grand Slam breakfast combo.

Contrary to popular belief, Justice isn't blind. **CHUCK NORRIS IS JUST THE ONLY PERSON SHE WANTS TO SEE.**

Chuck Norris bought the land for his ranch from Donald Trump for a handful of beads.

World War I was started after Chuck Norris decided there were too many goddamn people in Europe.

In Chinese ideograms, the symbol for Chuck Norris is comprised of the character for "justice" and the character for "boots."

Chuck Norris once passed a kidney stone in the shape and size of William Shatner, which sold at auction for $7 million.

Chuck Norris's fallout shelter contains four hundred cans of Spam, thirty cases of Johnnie Walker Red, and six Total Gyms.

Chuck Norris combs his beard with a brush made of Na'vi hair.

Chuck Norris was banned from *Fox and Friends* after his beard was found making out with Geraldo Rivera's mustache in the greenroom.

Chuck Norris's body odor smells like teen spirit.

Chuck Norris can play a perfect rendition of Gustav Holst's *The Planets* on a comb covered with a Kleenex.

Chuck Norris's backyard barbecue grill is used to cook every hot dog sold at Houston Astros home games.

Chuck Norris invented heavy metal music after Led Zeppelin asked him to build a guitar out of a solid block of iron.

Chuck Norris stopped telling jokes when he got tired of people laughing out of nervousness.

President Nixon was forced to resign when he learned Chuck Norris considered him "too goddamn liberal."

Chuck Norris likes his coffee the way he likes his justice: **INSTANT.**

If Chuck Norris asks you for a Shirley Temple, he will be expecting a children's musical on DVD, a handle of Maker's Mark, and an ambassadorship to Ghana in twenty-five years.

A Kevlar bathing suit is required attire if Chuck Norris ever invites you over to "shoot some pool."

Beethoven's "Symphony No. 9 in D minor" was composed after he read a story about a bearded commando in the jungles of Vietnam.

Chuck Norris must reapply every five years to renew his license to mess with Texas.

Chuck Norris knows an astounding magic trick where he asks you to pick a card and then punches you in the solar plexus.

The sight of raisins angers Chuck Norris because he knows they could have been made into Mad Dog 20/20.

Since 1984, all of Keith Richards's blood has been provided by Chuck Norris.

When Chuck Norris says, "Fuck you and the horse you rode in on," he's announcing his intentions.

ON

The next *Mission: Impossible* is rumored to be about Tom Cruise trying to convert Chuck Norris to Scientology.

At their wedding, Chuck Norris and his wife wrote their own vows. She promised to love, honor, and cherish him. He vowed to bring a world of pain to Jim Wertman of Groton, Connecticut. Chuck Norris is a man of his vows.

Chuck Norris destroyed Rainforest Cafe to launch an international logging operation.

Chuck Norris's brief career as a professional narcotics investigator ended after internal affairs raised suspicions about the high number of boot prints admitted into evidence at the crime scenes of the cases he closed.

Chuck Norris was asked to leave the reservation after an unfortunate incident in which he misheard the word "wampum."

After a grueling fifteen-minute interview, Chuck Norris drove Nancy Grace to suicide in a ten-foot ditch in the Appalachian woodlands, thirty miles from the nearest town.

Werner Heisenberg discovered his uncertainty principle when he realized it was impossible to determine both where Chuck Norris's fist was and how fast it was moving at the same time.

In the interest of public safety, the state of Oregon banned the sale of Volkswagens after Chuck Norris learned the "punch buggy" game.

The Experience Music Project in Seattle was closed for three weeks after Chuck Norris's visit when he wanted to experience oral sex with a life-size wax statue of Susan Boyle.

The only thing Congress can agree about on health care is recognizing Chuck Norris as the only legal form of euthanasia.

The safest sex Chuck Norris can get is with a Volvo.

Chuck Norris once made David Copperfield disappear by staring at him and telling him to get the fuck off his lawn.

The American Museum of Natural History abandoned plans for an exhibit called The Conquests of Chuck Norris when they realized Chuck Norris has never left anything standing for them to display.

In 1929, the United States Mint announced Chuck Norris would be featured on the dime. They quickly changed it back to the head of Mercury after the Chuck Norris dime became worth $4,000, plunging America into the Great Depression.

The first test for hostage negotiators in training is to convince Chuck Norris to vote Democrat. It is an exercise in learning to deal with defeat.

The lyrics to "LoveGame" are taken from a Valentine's Day card sent from Lady Gaga to Chuck Norris.

Chuck Norris received two Purple Hearts in the War on Poverty.

Chuck Norris's temper is directly proportional to the number of episodes of *Jersey Shore*.

Chuck Norris caused the *Hindenburg* to erupt in flames upon landing as a warning to travelers to stay away from New Jersey.

Whenever Chuck Norris is witnessed committing a crime, the police take the description as "a twentysomething black male."

WANTED
"PEDO BEAR"
WANTED
$100,000 REWARD

Who do you think taught that JetBlue flight attendant how to leave a plane like that?

Chuck Norris and Dirk Benedict are the only surviving founders of the Best Names of the Eighties Club.

At any U.S. airport security checkpoint, you can ask a TSA agent to bring you to a separate security screening where Chuck Norris looks you in the eyes and dares you to walk past him with anything illegal.

Chuck Norris can boil water in ninety seconds with his microwave-emitting corneas.

Hitch your wagon to a star, unless that star happens to be Chuck Norris, in which case you probably ought to consider an alternate career.

The greatest trick the devil ever pulled was convincing Chuck Norris to give him the name and number for his accountant.

There's no "I" in team, but there is one in Chuck Norris. It's a fairly easy name to spell really.

Chuck Norris will soon be starting a new website called Chuckslist where you can sell anything you want to Chuck Norris in exchange for shares of News Corporation.

Motor Trend's award for best hybrid of 2010 was given to Chuck Norris for completing a triathlon.

The *Walker, Texas Ranger* video game was discontinued after Chuck Norris's character came out of the TV and killed three teenagers.

The concept of the smoke monster in *Lost* was based on an old home movie of Chuck Norris chasing communists through jungle brush.

Chuck Norris has routinely threatened to light his underwear on fire on board transcontinental flights for years without any problems.

Chuck Norris shops for cars based on their speed relative to the Batmobile.

Justin Bieber's entire head of hair was grown from a single strand of Chuck Norris's pubes.

Chuck Norris beat *Final Fantasy XIII* on an Atari 2600.

Chuck Norris owns enough black belts to circle the Earth eleven times.

In the 2010 elections, Chuck Norris literally won the House back for Republicans room by room, starting in the lobby.

Chuck Norris celebrates the Fourth of July every year by proclaiming his own independence and drinking an ice-cold beer from the skull of King George III.

Should you ever come across Chuck Norris in the woods, remember that he is probably just as afraid as you aren't.

When he retires, Chuck Norris plans to become a police officer and partner up with Steven Seagal, finally melding justice and confusion in a way previously thought by experts to be impossible.

Chuck Norris can be triggered to kill just by watching *Huckabee.*

Chuck Norris can rub any *Family Guy* DVD on his beard and instantly make it funny again the next time you watch it.

King George VI hired Lionel Logue as a speaking coach because Chuck Norris only taught him how to negotiate for a good deal on an F-150.

Chuck Norris keeps Four Loko on tap.
IN HIS TRUCK.

Chuck Norris inadvertently discovered cold fusion when he poured two beers into a single glass.

BEER
BEE
EER

A head-butt from Chuck Norris delivers the same force as a thirty-mile-per-hour car crash and the same surprise as triplets.

Chuck Norris has won both the annual camel fighting and beauty pageants in Selçuk, Turkey, for seven years in a row.

There are over six hundred miles of black belts inside Chuck Norris's home.

Chuck Norris keeps hundreds of lobbyists employed due to his sheer desire to have Congress officially rename global warming "Bieber Fever."

Chuck Norris's ringtone is the sound of the space shuttle taking off during an air raid drill.

"Don't Ask, Don't Tell" was originally standard military shorthand for "If the enemies don't ask, don't tell them Chuck Norris is here."

Chuck Norris was given the key to the city of Bozeman, Montana, after hijacking a plane full of tourists and landing it there.

Chuck Norris is planning to produce *Ocean's Fourteen*, a story about how he and thirteen partners plan to rob you of eighty-five minutes and $11.

Chuck Norris has been known to commandeer entire ocean liners with only determination and a harpoon gun.

Who do you think Steve Jobs paid to "arrange" that liver transplant?

Every year on his birthday, Chuck Norris closes his eyes, wishes his hardest to meet George Bush Sr., and blows out the candles.

Chuck Norris can eat enough burritos from Chipotle in a single sitting to fill four Olympic-size diving pools.

Chuck Norris's golf clubs are crafted from the bones of mastodons.

Economists closely monitor sales of Chuck Norris movies to determine the health of the global economy.

Chuck Norris left his first and only Iron and Wine concert very disappointed because there was no smelting or grapes.

Any Friday when Chuck Norris walks into a store expecting a deal is considered Black Friday.

The only reason Optimus Prime came back at the end of *Transformers 2* was because Chuck Norris had some replacement parts in his garage.

Chuck Norris was the first person to jump through a ring of fire **IN A CITY BUS.**

Chuck Norris's credit card earns miles with every pilot he shoots down.

Chuck Norris built a wind farm to power his chain of gas stations.

Actuaries worldwide agree that the least likely event to ever occur on Earth is Chuck Norris becoming really good friends with Tracy Morgan.

The English rock band Muse was funded by Chuck Norris's desire for something to listen to while riding horses on fire during his annual trip across the galaxy to Alpha Centauri.

Chuck Norris can get a girl's number while landing a 747, extinguishing a four-alarm fire, and knocking out her boyfriend, all at the same time.

Law & Order is a series of weekly hour-long reenactments of Chuck Norris's legendary career as the NYPD's finest police car.

Chuck Norris's portrait has killed more visitors than any other painting in the history of the Smithsonian National Portrait Gallery.

HANG TOUGH CHUCK

Chuck Norris was the first person to reach the North Pole **BY ELEVATOR.**

Chuck Norris owns a compass that always points in the direction of Sean Hannity.

Chuck Norris is so conservative that he won't even use his left hand.

Chuck Norris's childhood Halloween stories were adapted to film as *Saw I–IV*.

The difference between Chuck Norris and Listerine is that Chuck Norris fights bad breath and germs with his fists.

Chuck Norris is currently gathering signatures for a petition so he would be named president of the United States until Barack Obama can provide proof of citizenship.

Chuck Norris learned the hard way that if you feed Wolf Blitzer chocolate, his stomach will explode, killing him instantly.

It is illegal to shout "Fire!" in a crowded movie theater, but if you shout "Chuck Norris is here!" in a crowded movie theater, balloons will fall from the ceiling as you are presented with an oversize check for $25,000.

Chuck Norris avoids airport security lines by checking himself in as the plane.

In Chuck Norris's fantasy United Nations, the Security Council is run by Ronald Reagan, Ronald McDonald, and Ron Popeil.

Chuck Norris was the first person fired during the 2010 season of *Celebrity Apprentice* for destroying Greece's economy while having sex with Ivanka Trump.

Chuck Norris was the original construction worker in the Village People until he decided to start remodeling the studio while recording "Macho Man."

The only people who would object to Chuck Norris running the New York City schools would be the residents, students, and teachers.

Chuck Norris committed a dozen felonies just to be able to meet O. J. Simpson in person.

Chuck Norris commits armed robbery with other people's arms.

Every year Chuck Norris asks his doctor to vaccinate him for H1N1, tetanus, and the *Seinfeld* curse.

Chuck Norris won a Tony Award for hailing a cab on Broadway.

In August 2010, thirty-three Chilean miners lost a bet to Chuck Norris that they couldn't afford to pay.

Chuck Norris can take over the world **FASTER THAN A NEW COLDPLAY ALBUM.**

Chuck Norris can build a fleet of locomotives in the time between *The Early Show* and *The Late Show.*

The spurs on Chuck Norris's boots have a three-ton towing capacity.

Chuck Norris is who won first place in the Monopoly beauty contest.

Oprah loves Chuck Norris's books.

Chuck Norris will only drive a van if it has the American flag and a bald eagle airbrushed on the side.

Chuck Norris was asked to resign from the Weather Channel for only forecasting "destruction."

ther
nnel
ORECAST
TOTALLY
FUCKED

Glee was going to do a musical version of a Chuck Norris movie until they found out nobody could sing in the key of awesome.

Chuck Norris taught The Stig how to drive.

Each night before he goes to sleep, Chuck Norris calls Dick Cheney for a bedtime story about the invasion of Iraq.

Chuck Norris gets his flu shot, bird shot, and shots of Jägermeister in the same injection.

Dr. Drew spent 147 days in rehab recovering from Chuck Norris.

Drivers slow down on the highway near accidents to try to see if Chuck Norris is nearby.

Don't be surprised if you see Rick Sanchez, Juan Williams, and Chuck Norris cohost a news commentary show in the near future.

Chuck Norris once convinced a polar bear that global warming doesn't exist.

VH1's next reality show will be called *Saddle of Love with Chuck Norris*, where a dozen hormone-crazed women will spend thirteen weeks in a mansion fighting to the death for his pure amusement.

Chuck Norris can ripen a melon by squeezing it in his taint.

Chuck Norris doesn't need to sign up for Facebook to poke anybody.

Chuck Norris's immune system is **MORE EFFICIENT THAN AN INDONESIAN SWEATSHOP.**

Chuck Norris uses Gillette Stadium to shave his beard.

Chuck Norris Avenue in Los Angeles was renamed shortly after its dedication because nobody can cross Chuck Norris and live.

Chuck Norris routinely parks in front of fire hydrants when he drives his custom-made fire truck.

The Library of Congress has archived over thirty thousand different recordings of Chuck Norris reciting the Pledge of Allegiance.

Chuck Norris can prevent forest fires, but he's usually too busy creating them.

Chuck Norris once fell in love—then the mirror broke.

All bets are off—unless they're all on Chuck Norris.

When Chuck Norris claps with one hand, the sound is deafening.

Chuck Norris can destroy ten thousand acres of rain forest with a single sneeze.

Mona Lisa didn't smile before Chuck Norris spent a night in the Louvre.

Inception was written after Christopher Nolan watched Chuck Norris kill ten men in his sleep.

Brewers of Coors Light use Chuck Norris to tap the Rockies.

The Russians staged Chernobyl to cover up a Chuck Norris fart.

Chuck Norris's appliances don't need power buttons—just somewhere he can insert his penis.

The light at the end of the tunnel is Chuck Norris's fist rushing toward you.

Chuck Norris once played a game of Hearts and shot the moon, killing the entire Apollo space program.

Men are from Mars and women are from Venus, but Chuck Norris is from the United States of America, so men and women can go fuck themselves.

STR8
SHOOTER

A monument still stands in memory of the events of October 12, 1983, when Chuck Norris high-fived every single man, woman, and child in Biloxi, Mississippi.

Chuck Norris once actually made it rain cats and dogs just to take care of a mouse problem.

Every Tour de France winner has doped using Chuck Norris's blood.

LeBron James chose Miami to be near Chuck Norris's summer home.

When Chuck Norris compares apples to oranges, they are equivalent.

Chuck Norris holds an iPhone 4 **ANY WAY HE DAMN WELL CHOOSES.**

Area 51 is where Chuck Norris keeps his pets.

Animators invented CGI to try to do justice to Chuck Norris's beard.

Until Vatican II, the Bible was dedicated to "Chuck Norris's testicles, for making this all possible."

Chuck Norris once brushed his teeth and invented jazz fusion.

Chuck Norris arranged the Bay of Pigs invasion to distract JFK while he slept with Jackie O.

Chuck Norris found the goose that laid the golden eggs—then he killed it. Chuck Norris doesn't need handouts.

Grappa is what's left over in the cup when Chuck Norris visits the dentist.

Intelligent design exists because evolution can't explain how Chuck Norris was born as an ass-kicking machine.

Washington, D.C., gave up on a Chuck Norris monument after five women became pregnant just from looking at his genitals.

Barbie left Ken for Chuck Norris and his one-twelfth-scale Jeep Wrangler but went back to Ken when she couldn't deal with Chuck Norris's full-scale penis.

Conan O'Brien's coif is made from hair shaved off Chuck Norris's back.

Chuck Norris holds the record for fastest lap speed around the Nürburgring in a pontoon boat dragged by a brontosaurus.

The state of Kentucky was founded because Chuck Norris needed a place to hang out.

Chuck Norris has pockets sewn into his skin.

Edward and Jacob are on Team Chuck.

TEAM
CHUCK
TEAM
CHUCK

Chuck Norris did not guest-star on *Seinfeld* because you always know what the deal with Chuck Norris is.

Chuck Norris's nickname is Charles.

The Snuggie was invented after someone saw Chuck Norris watch *Walker, Texas Ranger* while wearing the skin of a bear he had dressed himself.

Chuck Norris kills people with kindness before killing them again with a roundhouse kick.

States that vote red are voting for Chuck Norris's beard.

Mormons keep high-quality genealogical records to prove that every member of their religion is descended from Chuck Norris.

Chuck Norris taught a bear to train a pack of wolves to raise a human boy.

Chuck Norris only carries money so he can bet on himself.

Peter Pan wants to stay a boy because he can't grow up to become Chuck Norris.

Memorial Day is a holiday weekend because it takes three days to read a list of all of Chuck Norris's victims.

Moses's encounter with the burning bush was actually a conversation with the pubic area of a woman Chuck Norris had just boned.

Shaquille O'Neal wears Chuck Norris's baby shoes during games.

At rock concerts, Chuck Norris plugs his ears with live kittens.

Chuck Norris was once on a 747 that crashed. Even though rescue teams got to the wreckage within fifteen minutes, Chuck Norris had already eaten all the other survivors.

“The Land of Milk and Honey” is Chuck Norris’s nickname for his pectoral muscles.

Lawyers at the studio behind *Walker, Texas Ranger* won't let them rerelease it in 3-D because of the certainty of millions of dollars in accidental-death lawsuit settlements.

Chuck Norris only knows how to kiss one way—
WITH THE KISS OF DEATH.

Chuck Norris built the railroads with his own two hands, making tracks from shavings taken from his testicles.

When told to talk to the hand, Chuck Norris ripped it off and used it to judo-chop its original owner.

Chuck Norris is the first person on the Ghostbusters' speed dial.

Chuck Norris can finish other people's sentences with his fist.

Chuck Norris does the *New York Times* crossword puzzle **IN BLOOD.**

Every punch Chuck Norris throws hits the strike zone.

On subway cars, the closing doors stand clear of Chuck Norris.

Chuck Norris's plan for Middle East peace is to airdrop Total Gyms for every man, woman, and child across the entire region until there are no more complaints.

total gym

Chuck Norris's penis has a license to thrill.

The *Cloud Gate* sculpture in Chicago's Millennium Park is on loan from Chuck Norris's scrotum.

In 2008, Chuck Norris started an NGO to relieve Colombian drug cartels of their teeth.

Chuck Norris sweats the Force.

Chuck Norris is the only signatory to the laws of nature.

Chuck Norris trained an army of zombies to defend themselves against a robot uprising.

Chuck Norris kills vampires simply by crossing his fingers.

If Chuck Norris is ever disappointed with his writing, he crumples up his monitor and throws it away.

Only God has the authority to edit Chuck Norris's Wikipedia page.

Chuck Norris can heal a head wound with his thoughts.

Chuck Norris turned down the chance to play James Bond because the weapons took all the fun out of the killing.

Chuck Norris can ignore the call of nature for up to thirty-six hours, but he can never ignore the call of duty.

A reporter once asked Chuck Norris what was on his mind; Chuck Norris removed the top of his skull, bent down to display his brain matter, and then replaced his pate.

Chuck Norris once swallowed a python to get to the live deer in its stomach.

George Clooney is still single because he's holding out for Chuck Norris.

Chuck Norris supports debt relief. He believes people should be comfortable before he kills them.

Chuck Norris hates Wall Street fat cats, but he loves how they taste in stews.

To reach the front door of Chuck Norris's house, you must cross a moat on the night of a new moon, tunnel precisely 32.6 meters beneath the earth, answer the gorgon's 16 riddles in ancient Greek, cross a burning rope bridge hundreds of feet above a river of burning lava, and avoid the fighting colonies of irradiated soldier ants. And if you get past the land mines, the door is unlocked.

Chuck Norris plays the castanets by checking himself for testicular cancer.

Chuck Norris can synchronize his urination with the fountains at the Bellagio.

Nintendo changed *Chuck Norris's Punch-Out!!* to *Mike Tyson's Punch-Out!!* because of complaints that the last level was unbeatable.

When Chuck Norris covers his eyes during peekaboo, babies disappear forever.

When a Chuck Norris movie bombs, an average of 323 people die in the aftermath.

Chuck Norris has killed eighty-seven mimes with one invisible shotgun.

Chuck Norris's beard is space's final frontier.

Chuck Norris uses a hollowed-out elephant trunk as a holster for his penis.

When Chuck Norris raises his eyebrows, mating season begins around the world.

At Chuck Norris's circumcision, doctors ran through five diamond-studded chain saws before giving up.

The movie *Hellraiser* is based on real-life events that occurred after someone tried to solve the *Chuck Norris: Karate Kommandos* Special Edition Rubik's Cube.

Chuck Norris's children were born fully bearded.

Chuck Norris stalked, captured, killed, and ate his own shadow because it was working for the KGB.

The Irish Potato Famine started when Chuck Norris had a hankering for latkes.

Chuck Norris once fucked a stripper without breaking through the fake birthday cake.

Chuck Norris has sired a Kentucky Derby champion and its jockey.

Chuck Norris feels your pain as an explosion of anger directed at your face.

Chuck Norris is a conservative; he understands the need to conserve his energy to kick as many liberal asses as possible.

Chuck Norris has settled every case brought against him by offering the aggrieved party a single hair from his beard.

Chuck Norris's friends with benefits have the benefit of not being his enemies.

Chuck Norris invented the water bed after his first wet dream.

Chuck Norris does not hang up on people; he just hangs them.

When Chuck Norris takes a shower, the leftover water is 68 percent alcohol by volume.

Chuck Norris coached a vending machine to win a speed skating tournament.

People who live in glass houses shouldn't throw stones unless they're positive that Chuck Norris is nowhere nearby and would be highly unlikely to ever catch wind of the incident.

The leopard does not change his spots, but Chuck Norris changes out of his leopard-skin thongs often enough to keep them smelling presentable.

Imitation is the sincerest form of flattery, but imitation of Chuck Norris will only get you flattened.

The opera ain't over till the fat lady sings or Chuck Norris decapitates the chorus, which turns out to have been goons from the Japanese Yakuza in disguise.

There's none so blind as those who will not see, except for those whose eyes have been forced from their skulls by a scissor kick to the temple from Chuck Norris.

Blood is thicker than water, **EXCEPT FOR THE WATER IN CHUCK NORRIS'S TEAR DUCTS,** which have petrified into diamonds from decades of disuse.

Appearances are deceptive. Most people assume Chuck Norris can chew through steel; this is true, but only because his lavalike saliva renders it quite soft.

Chuck Norris carries a midget in his pocket—after Chuck kicks ass, the midget takes names.

Good fences make good neighbors, but since Chuck Norris's neighbors couldn't afford a steel-reinforced replica of the Great Wall of China, they make him fresh cookies every day.

Chuck Norris doesn't use Twitter because nobody can follow Chuck Norris and survive.

Chuck Norris designed the first Ed Hardy T-shirt when he ran out of douchebags to kill.

Chuck Norris's mug just says "World's Best."

What happens in Vegas stays in Vegas. Unless it was a Chuck Norris roundhouse kick to the face. That shit stays with you for life. If you live.

Chuck Norris invented the muffin when he wanted a cupcake for breakfast.

Chuck Norris has a birthmark in the shape of Chuck Norris kicking a ninja.

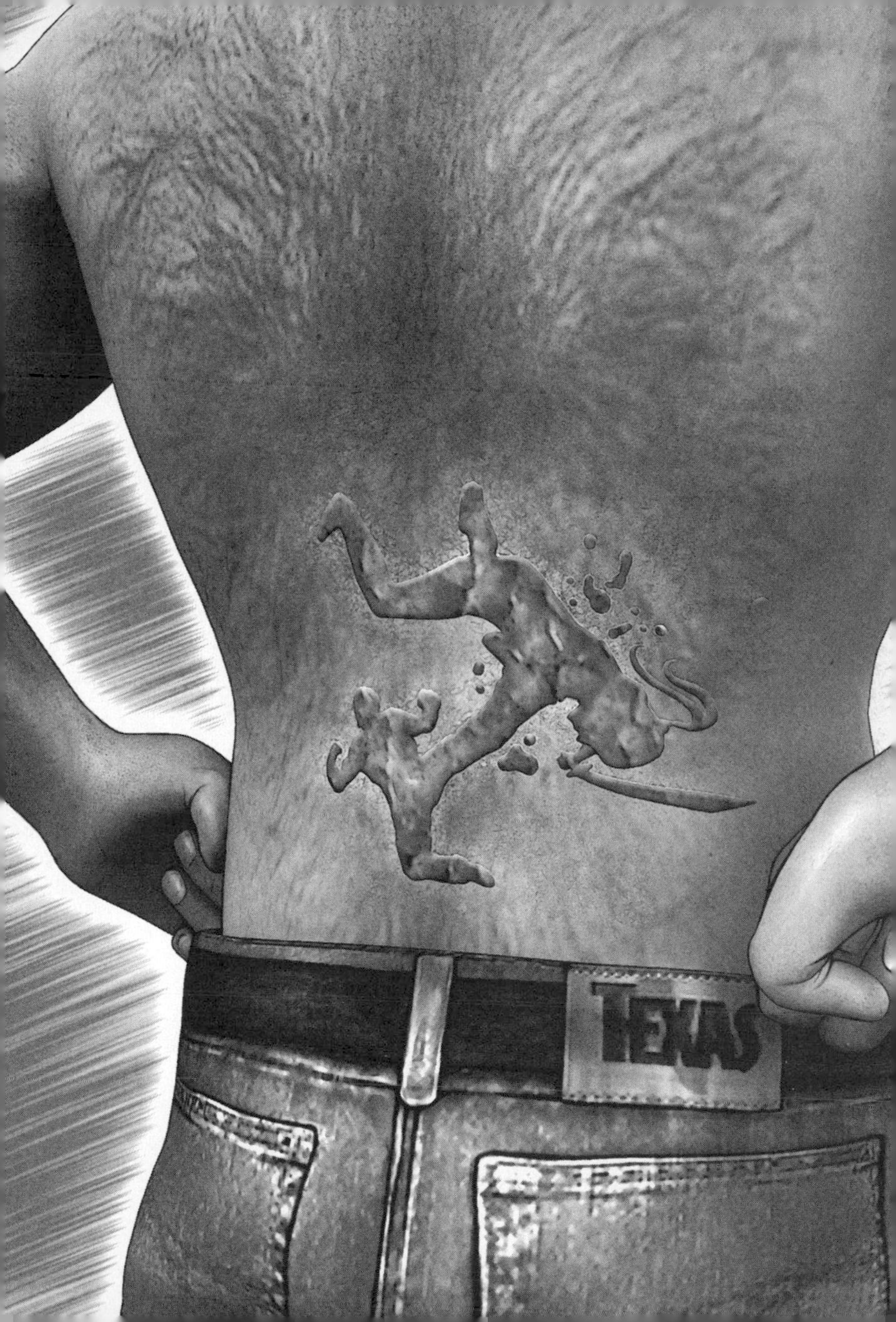
TEXAS

Chuck Norris always gives his seat to pregnant women on the train but never apologizes for getting them pregnant.

Chuck Norris goes to the gun range so the targets can practice running from him.

Chuck Norris can recite pi backward.

Astronauts dream of becoming Chuck Norris when they grow up.

"B.C." actually stands for "Before Chuck."

When Chuck Norris goes to the bathroom, he doesn't take a shit, he gives a shit.

Two roads diverged in a yellow wood because Chuck Norris told them to.

Chuck Norris's first coloring book was the *Kama Sutra.*

Chuck Norris calls out his own name during sex because anything else would ruin the moment.

Chuck Norris has no sense of self-preservation except for when he's making a batch of his award-winning jams.

Chuck Norris's legs, Law and Order, are currently serving a life sentence for killing Dharma and Greg.

When, as a child, he was placed on Santa Claus's lap for a photo, Chuck Norris shat out Donner, Blitzen, and four other reindeer.

When filling out a job application, Chuck Norris fills in his race as "superior."

Chuck Norris has actually lifted Texas by its panhandle.

Chuck Norris waterboards himself to clear his sinuses.

Chuck Norris traced his ancestry back to Chuck Norris.

Chuck Norris can sing a solo in perfect three-part harmony.

Chuck Norris can win a three-legged race by himself.

Che Guevara was buried wearing a shirt with Chuck Norris on it.

Chuck Norris was the best man at his own wedding.

There is no comeback for an insult from Chuck Norris. Then again, if Chuck Norris wanted some comeback, he would have asked your mom for it.

Chuck Norris owns a Swiss Army knife that contains a colander, a flamethrower, and a Snuggie.

Chuck Norris's first solution for the cholera outbreak in Haiti was another earthquake.

Chuck Norris took Gary Coleman to small-claims court just for the irony.

Chuck Norris's favorite Bond girl is the tank from *GoldenEye.*

Chuck Norris uses **ENTIRE BOOKS** as bookmarks.

As a good Christian, Chuck Norris ought to forgive anyone for wrongdoings against him. Unfortunately, Chuck Norris retains Jewish attorneys, so good luck with that.

A massive avalanche in the Kohistan District of Pakistan in February 2010 killed over one hundred people. Coincidentally, it occurred at the exact instant that Chuck Norris heard about plans for an Islamic cultural center blocks from Ground Zero.

Chuck Norris is all for government bailouts so long as repayment is enforced by Dog the Bounty Hunter.

Tony Stark made an iron man suit for Chuck Norris, but Chuck has never used it because it only slows him down.

The only papers WikiLeaks have on Chuck Norris just have "Fuck you, Dan Rather" written on them in blood.

Chuck Norris uses the same octane gasoline in his car, lawn mower, and martinis.

Chuck Norris was the first to install a fireplace in an igloo.

As a young man, Chuck Norris wore the pants in every relationship he was in to the point where he refused to let his girlfriend even own pants.

The last person Chuck Norris blew out of the water died from the bends.

You can find Chuck Norris at Costco, Walmart, or any retailer where firearms, power tools, knives, duct tape, Vaseline, and Fritos are sold.

Church fathers edited out the part of the Gospel where Chuck Norris rappelled into the Last Supper, karate-chopped the table, and teabagged Judas.

Chuck Norris's underwear can resist continuous gunfire for up to twenty-four hours.

Chuck Norris's most prized possession is his signed copy of the 1993 *Women of the U.S. Attorney's Office* commemorative wall calendar.

Chuck Norris called GEICO and in fifteen minutes saved fifteen senior citizens from a blazing building before convincing the phone representative to donate $10,000 to the Republican Party.

Chuck Norris and his brother cracked four of Bob Barker's ribs while teaching him karate. Read that again because it is *actually true*.

The Swedish invented IKEA so they could spend less time building furniture and more time running from Chuck Norris and his deep displeasure with the Bauhaus style and European modernism.

Every scene from *Life* and *Planet Earth* was filmed in Chuck Norris's pants.

Chuck Norris spent an entire month jumping off high-rise buildings intending to marry the first woman who could catch him.

Chuck Norris can tell the difference between Pepsi and RC Cola, but he has yet to use this skill.

Chuck Norris won a People's Choice Award for winning a knife fight against Joe Biden.

Chuck Norris calls 411 every day at noon asking for the latest updates on the Soviets.

Emperor Nero paid Chuck Norris sacks of gold and silver to burn Rome to the ground. Chuck Norris accepted because that buys a lot of whey powder.

Chuck Norris refuses to see *The Social Network* because he's had five hundred million friends since 1972.

Chuck Norris's storm cellar contains a tunnel that leads you directly to Sydney, Australia.

In a direct-to-DVD sequel to the animated classic, Chuck Norris plays the eighth dwarf, Murdery, who bangs Snow White.

Chuck Norris's beard glows red when he proves a syllogism.

The lightbulbs in Chuck Norris's house are replaced every day because nobody wants to run the risk of getting stuck in the dark with Chuck Norris.

Chuck Norris once delivered a performance so stiff that a cameraman was later pulled over for DWI.

At one crossroad in his life, Chuck Norris considered becoming an obstetrician and a postman so he could deliver newborns by mail.

Every summer, Chuck Norris invites the remaining cast members of *The Partridge Family* and *The Brady Bunch* to a fight to the death inside an active volcano.

If you ever get Chuck Norris's voice mail, the greeting will be, "Hello. I am not available to take your call right now **BECAUSE I AM IN YOUR HOUSE."**

Chuck Norris once competed in a celebrity edition of the game show *The Weakest Link* that went to sudden death. There were fourteen casualties.

Chuck Norris's favorite power lunch is a dozen nine-volt batteries.

Chuck Norris's first words were the opening speech from *Patton*.

To be more environmentally conscious, Chuck Norris retrofitted his pickup truck to run on Toyota Priuses.

In the late eighties, Chuck Norris once roundhouse-kicked Michael Jackson so hard, he knocked all the black off him.

Conspiracy theorists are skeptical of the 9/11 attack on the Pentagon because the damage looks awfully similar to the destruction left by Chuck Norris when he destroyed the Hexagon, Trapezoid, and Parallelogram buildings.

Chuck Norris is sharp enough to cut a tin can in half and can slice a tomato paper-thin.

Chuck Norris won a spelling bee by filling the judges' pants with a thousand angry wasps.

Chuck Norris's refrigerator can keep milk fresh longer than most relationships last.

Chuck Norris can have an all-you-can-eat buffet delivered.

Chuck Norris was captain of the Love Boat until one day when everyone woke up and saw they were in Pyongyang.

Chuck Norris will only send letters in envelopes made of chain mail.

Chuck Norris's ant farm is the third-highest producer of grain in the Midwest.

Chuck Norris's full legal name is Carlos Danger de Saavedra Sixth Duke of Atlantis Death Rattle degli Alighieri Ray Hohenzollern Saxe-Coburg and Gotha, Supreme Underwater Commando, Protector of the Second Amendment Norris.

Chuck Norris is the highest-paid model in Hungary.

Chuck Norris once fell out of a fourteen-story window into love.

Chuck Norris only wears suits made from the finest Italian marble.

Chuck Norris can make origami with his foldout couch.

People who are antiunion are just afraid of the thought of Chuck Norris striking anything.

Chuck Norris's social security is knowing that society will continue to exist so long as he's around.

Mike Tyson has a standing invitation to any of Chuck Norris's renowned banquets made entirely from human ears.

Chuck Norris's orthodox stance has been certified kosher by the Central Rabbinical Congress of the United States and Canada.

The 1977 film *Breaker! Breaker!* stars Chuck Norris as a truck driver who literally destroys an entire town using only eighteen-wheelers.

Chuck Norris operates the largest fire-breathing dragon farm.

Chuck Norris has had sex in every U.S. embassy in the Northern Hemisphere.

Chuck Norris isn't really a cat person, which is why he only has one lion.

Chuck Norris sent one of his children to Guantánamo for three months for not taking out the trash.

Chuck Norris is the patron saint of patron saints.

Doctors debate the nutritional benefits of the Chuck Norris Salad because it only contains ten pounds of raw beef, one head of lettuce, and two heads of state.

Chuck Norris's preferred golf cart is a monster truck called the Violator.

Chuck Norris once destroyed over one thousand panes of glass in the NorthPark Center mall in Dallas, Texas, merely by window-shopping.

Chuck Norris can commit a fatal hit-and-run on foot.

Chuck Norris can turn a walrus inside out with his bare hands.

ACKNOWLEDGMENTS

Illustrations:
Angelo Vildasol

Special thanks to:
Kevin Allison, Joe Bianco, Dave Bourla,
and Tony Caroselli

ABOUT THE AUTHOR

Ian Spector started the web phenomenon "Chuck Norris Facts" back in 2005 and is the *New York Times* bestselling author of *The Truth About Chuck Norris, Chuck Norris vs. Mr. T,* and *Chuck Norris Cannot Be Stopped.* Ian is a graduate of Brown University, where he studied cognitive neuroscience, edited the campus humor magazine, and served as the president of the Brown Entrepreneurship Program. He is currently living in Manhattan running a social technology start-up and is a freelance digital strategy consultant. You can see what he's up to and get in touch at IanJSpector.com or follow @IanJSpector on Twitter.